Collectib'
RABBI'S

Herbert N. Schiffer

Schiffer Publishing Ltd

1469 Morstein Road, West Chester, Pennsylvania 19380

This work is dedicated to Mary Lou Holt for her kindly given help. I would like thank my grandparents, Migs and Jim Nutt, and Herbert and Margaret Schiffer, for their encouragement. I am grateful to the managers of the Brimfield Associates Inc., who arranged for me to take pictures at the Atlantique City market. My thanks go to Tim Scott and the others at Schiffer Publishing.

I became interested in rabbits when I got a pair and started to sell the babies. After a short time I started to really like the idea of rabbits because most of the time they bring happiness into people's lives.

The rabbits also have made me more in touch with animals because they were always some of my best friends and they have been a source of enjoyment to me. The rabbits have made me nicer to different things that are warm and fluffy and nice to different people.

I started to collect rabbit-oriented objects soon after I had my first rabbit. My grandmother encouraged me to collect different kinds of things, mainly rabbits.

Title page photo:
Cloth cut-out rabbit. Paper box depicting rabbits. Tin Easter egg with a rabbit in the decoration. Cup and saucer of tin with *Wind in the Willows* decoration. One-foot ruler with a parade of rabbits. *Mary Lou Holt collection.*

Copyright © 1990 by Herbert N. Schiffer.
Library of Congress Catalog Number: 90-61744.

Printed in the United States of America.
ISBN: 0-88740-268-2

Published by Schiffer Publishing, Ltd.
1469 Morstein Road
West Chester, Pennsylvania 19380
Please write for a free catalog.
This book may be purchased from the publisher.
Please include $2.00 postage.
Try your bookstore first.

Contents

Pink plastic trailer attached to a pink plastic rabbit. Plastic face in plush rabbit suit. Cloth rabbit driving cloth carrot car. Plush rabbit eating carrot. *Mary Lou Holt collection.*

Plush rabbit dressed in shirt and pants with a cloth cut-out rabbit in a tin cart pulled by tin rabbit. *Mary Lou Holt collection.*

Papier-mâché and Staffordshire ceramic rabbits posing for a picture in the desert. *Margaret Schiffer collection.*

Metal Rabbits

Rabbit in overalls pushing wheelbarrow. *Debrah Holt.*

Formal rabbit door stop. *Private collection.*

Tin figures and Easter eggs with two Lehman toys. *Margaret Schiffer collection.*

Cast brass pieces. *Private collection.*

Two cast iron rabbit door stops. *Margaret Schiffer collection.*

Metal match holder with striker. *Debrah Holt.*

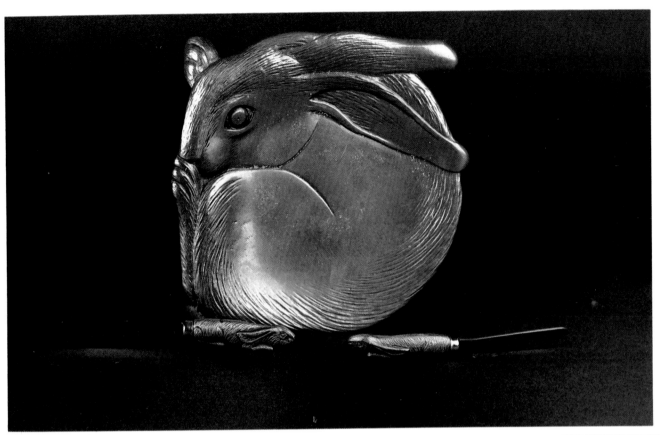

Serving dish in the form of a crouching mother rabbit and her young are depicted as cheese knives. *Mary Lou Holt collection.*

Metal serving dish with a spoon. *Debrah Holt.*

Napkin holder with engraving and spoon. *Private collection.*

Child's tin lunch pails and covered containers. *Mary Lou Holt collection.*

Tin child's plates and container. *Mary Lou Holt collection.*

Tin child's tray with rabbit border. *Mary Lou Holt collection.*

Square tray depicting rabbits. *Mary Lou Holt collection.*

Two nineteenth-century cast iron doorstops. *Margaret Schiffer collection.*

Tin child's lunch pail, top view. *Bierdman collection.*

Same pail but different view. *Bierdman collection.*

Opposite page top:
Two tin toys, purse, and one circular container. *Mary Lou Holt collection.*

Bottom:
Rabbit picture drawn on top of a container. *Private collection.*

Tin peanut container. *Bierdman collection.*

Tin toffee container. *Bierdman collection.*

BUNNIES ON A PICNIC

MRS. STEVEN'S CHICAGO

HOME MADE CANDIES

Chocolate mold of one rabbit on a pedestal. *Private collection.*

Metal chocolate mold in the form of one standing rabbit. *Private collection.*

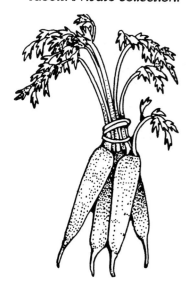

Chocolate rabbit mold for two rabbits carrying baskets, 13¼" H, 9" W. *The Book Shelf.*

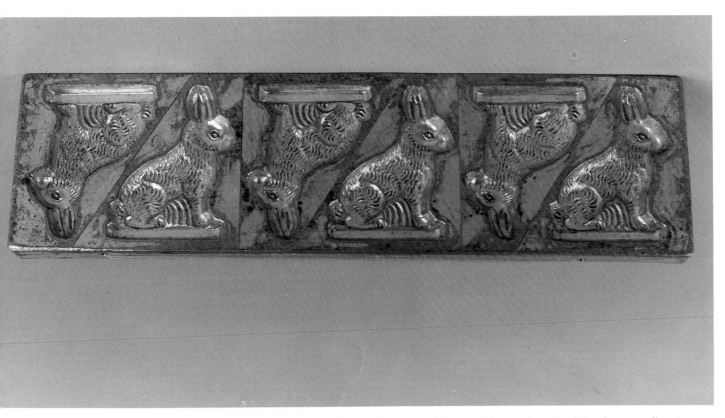

Chocolate mold made for six rabbits on flat pedestals. *Bierdman collection.*

Four chocolate molds for one rabbit each. *Bierdman collection.*

Ceramic Rabbits

Wedgwood plates, 1980s, Peter Rabbit. *Private collection.*

Rabbit platter, English, 1900s. *Joyce Leiby.*

Opposite page:
Cast rabbits on lettuce head and carrot. *Mary Lou Holt collection.*

Salt and pepper shakers. *Debrah Holt*.

Ceramic teapot 1945-1950, made in the U.S. zone in Germany. *Joyce Leiby*.

Honey and jelly pot with rabbit lids. *Private collection*.

Butter container with knives. *Mary Lou Holt collection.*

One cast ceramic vase and three other cast rabbits. *Mary Lou Holt collection.*

Four chalkware rabbits all in simple flat bases. *Margaret Schiffer collection.*

Humongous Japanese Imari porcelain rabbit figure and his dwarf friend, a Japanese rabbit incense holder, porcelain, nineteenth century. *Private collection.*

Ceramic rabbit in sitting position. *Margaret Schiffer collection.*

Ceramic Easter egg with rabbit painting on the front. *Mary Lou Holt collection.*

Glass Rabbits

Glass rabbit in a basket. *Mary Lou Holt collection*.

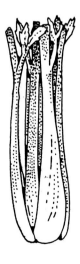

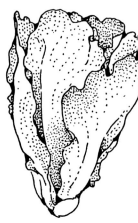

Glass Christmas ornament. *Private collection.*

Three glass candy containers. *Bierdman collection.*

Glass rabbit in basket carrying a basket. *Mary Lou Holt collection.*

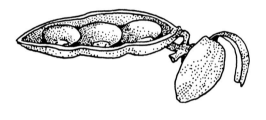

Three glass rabbits in the form of candy containers. *Bierdman collection.*

Three glass candy container rabbits. *Lare.*

Multiple candy container rabbits of varying shapes and sizes. *Mary Lou Holt collection.*

Young girls dressed in bunny suits. *Mary Lou Holt collection.*

Plastic Rabbits

Small cute faces on rabbit figures. *Mary Lou Holt collection.*

Three plastic rabbits in cute pose. *Private collection.*

Three rabbits conversing with one another. *Mary Lou Holt collection.*

Two rabbits together, one is doing a split. *Mary Lou Holt collection.*

Three working bunnies talking together. *Mary Lou Holt collection.*

Two rabbits going off to work, one has a wheelbarrow and the other a basket. *Mary Lou Holt collection.*

Twentieth-century Japanese celluloid rabbit grouping. *Margaret Schiffer collection.*

Four plastic rabbits all leaving from work. *Mary Lou Holt collection.*

Three plastic rabbits playfully going to the country. *Mary Lou Holt collection.*

Two plastic rabbits talking on the way to work. *Mary Lou Holt collection.*

Four rabbits trudging across the yard. *Mary Lou Holt collection.*

Four rabbits conversing together. *Mary Lou Holt collection.*

Four rabbits going to the carrot field. *Mary Lou Holt collection.*

Five rabbits trying to figure out the answer to a problem. *Mary Lou Holt collection.*

Three separate ways that these rabbits get around. *Mary Lou Holt collection.*

Three rabbits going to the nearest farm with Easter eggs. *Mary Lou Holt collection.*

Three rabbits deciding where to place an Easter egg. *Mary Lou Holt collection.*

Two boats on a pond with the owner's cars off to the side on the bank. *Mary Lou Holt collection.*

Five rabbits all going to their own separate places. *Debrah Holt.*

Four Easter eggs all in a row. *Mary Lou Holt collection.*

Three rabbits collecting Easter eggs. *Mary Lou Holt collection.*

A plastic toy car and a plastic Easter container. *Mary Lou Holt collection.*

Six plastic figures in a semicircle. *Private collection.*

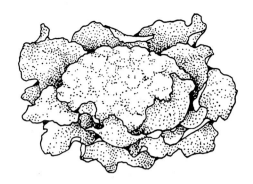

Plastic roly-poly rabbit with its original box.

One formal rabbit toy and one funny-looking toy with large pink wheels. *Mary Lou Holt collection.*

Two rabbits that live in shoes. *Mary Lou Holt collection.*

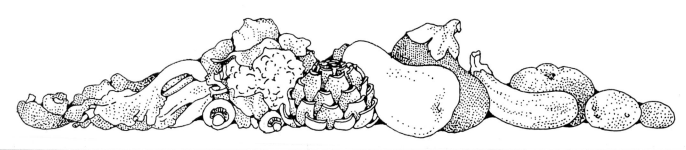

Two cute custom Southern Belles made by Kim Nelson Prescot. *Ben & Carol Nelson Antiques.*

Cloth Rabbits

Uncle Wiggly rabbit without most of his original clothes. *Cynthia's Country Store, Inc.*

Uncle Wiggly with most of his original cloths and markings. *Old Friends Antiques.*

Warner Brothers' Bugs Bunny, 1940-1950. *Mimi's Memories.*

Two cloth figures. *Margaret Schiffer collection.*

Stuffed and sewn rabbit figure. *Private collection.*

Theorem painted velvet rabbit, 1880-1900. *Joyce Leiby.*

1925 rabbit pull toy. *Joyce Leiby.*

Two stuffed rabbits conversing together. *Mary Lou Holt collection.*

Washer woman rabbit, German candy container. *Joyce Leiby.*

Nine rabbits (of ten) that are part of a game that is like bowling. *Margaret Schiffer collection.*

Rabbit running along to greet his friends with a snack. *Mary Lou Holt collection.*

Two cloth cut-out rabbits that have been stuffed. *Mary Lou Holt collection.*

Three young schoolboys staying in line, all ready for a new day. *Mary Lou Holt collection.*

Four needlework rabbits made by Margaret B. Schiffer, 1980s. *Margaret Schiffer collection.*

Marionette rabbit that is still in fairly good condition. *Mimi's Memories.*

Two pillows made by Margaret B. Schiffer, 1980s. *Margaret Schiffer collection.*

39

Two West German rabbits at school; the rabbits go up and down on a motorized mechanism. *Carousel Antique Mall.*

Plush Rabbits

Two plush rabbits, one has a pink cloth dress and the other a pink bow around his neck. *Mary Lou Holt collection.*

Seven plush rabbits from the 1800s. *Margaret Schiffer collection.*

A family of rabbits with the father in a sailor costume, one is in a formal coat, and the other is in a polka-dotted dress and apron. *Mary Lou Holt collection.*

Stuffed sailor rabbit with two models of seagoing vessels. *Mary Lou Holt collection.*

Stuffed marching military officer rabbit. *Private collection.*

A prominent rabbit in his community and a military rabbit talking about the future. *Mary Lou Holt collection.*

A bandleader telling another rabbit where he is supposed to be. *Mary Lou Holt collection.*

This soldier rabbit appears to be looking for his unit.

A fashion rabbit showing off the newest style. *Private collection.*

Three plush nodding-head rabbits. *Private collection.*

Three plush Steiff rabbits discussing whose carrot patch they will raid next. *Lil' David's Wood Box.*

A long-eared rabbit who is trying to stay calm for his picture. *Private collection.*

European nodding-head rabbit with basket. *Scott Tagliapietra.*

Two inspectors with the traditional clothing. This is a husband and wife team. *Mary Lou Holt collection.*

Two stuffed rabbits from the 1950s. *Lil' David's Wood Box.*

Wilfred, an English rabbit, from the 1920s-1930s. *Barbara and Bob Lauver.*

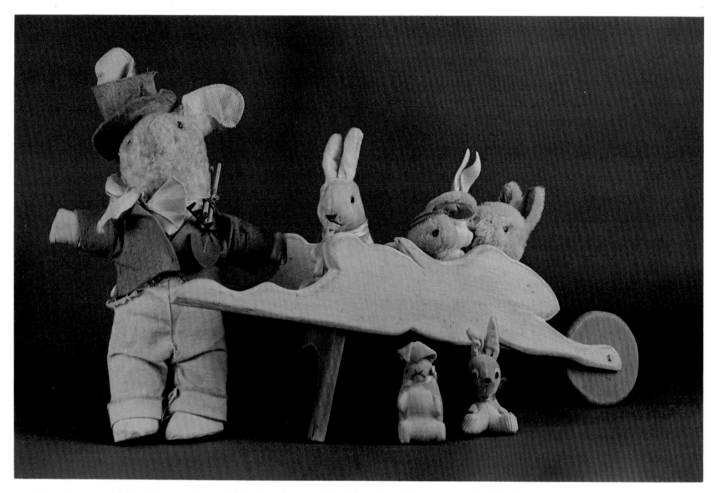

Gardener rabbit with smaller rabbits in the cart that he is pulling around with him. *Mary Lou Holt collection.*

A lazy rabbit talking with his other rabbit friends. *Private collection.*

Opposite page: Wolf in a rabbit suit who is trying to get his meals for that day. *Mary Lou Holt collection.*

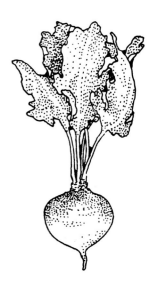

A rabbit on a wind-up vehicle with a basket on his back. *Joyce McClelland.*

Two worker rabbits, both with baskets on their backs. *Mary Lou Holt collection.*

Opposite page: A candy container rabbit on a sled. *Scott Tagliapietra.*

Opposite page:
A large rabbit mask. *Hadley Antiques Center.*

Above:
Chef rabbit with his favorite stew pot. *Mary Lou Holt collection.*

Left:
1950s Schuco rabbit with yes-no mechanism. *Joyce McClelland.*

Two rabbits with a baby in a little rabbit costume. *Mary Lou Holt collection.*

Six stuffed rabbits who are all good friends. *Mary Lou Holt collection.*

Two candy container rabbits, one is of simple construction and the other more difficult. *Mary Lou Holt collection.*

Three rabbits standing in a line. *Mary Lou Holt collection.*

Steiff rabbit who is on wheels that wobble side to side when it is pulled along. *Mimi's Memories.*

Steiff rabbit from about 1950s. He is on a little cart that wobbles as it goes. *Barbara and Bob Lauver.*

53

Four rabbits who enjoy talking together. *Mary Lou Holt collection.*

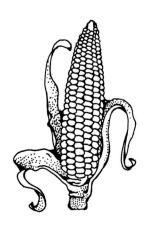

A Steiff rabbit who is dressed in a German outfit and his young friend. *Bunny Walker.*

54

Two plush rabbits who are just hanging around. *Mary Lou Holt collection.*

Three separate figures that make a set. The rabbits all appear to be looking in the bird cage with the birds in it. *Private collection.*

Four rabbits, two blue, two pink, and all have a personality all their own. *Mary Lou Holt collection.*

One Easter rabbit who is sleeping after a long run carrying an egg. *Private collection.*

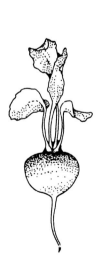

Many rabbits and many colors to go along with the multiple shapes. *Mary Lou Holt collection.*

Another stuffed sleeping Easter bunny with his egg. *Private collection.*

A Wild West show with a cowbunny dressed as a cowboy and an elephant instead of a cow. *Mary Lou Holt collection.*

Six rabbits, all of different sizes and shapes. *Mary Lou Holt collection.*

A rabbit who is carrying a basket and some chicks that are trying to use the basket as a perch. *Private collection.*

A little rabbit that is being used as a horse. *Private collection.*

Three young rabbits are all friends and they want their picture taken. *Lil' David's Wood Box*.

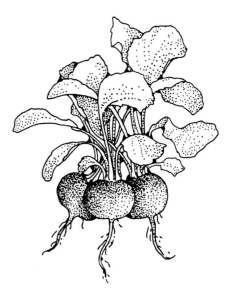

Three rabbits that are telling jokes to one another. *Private collection*.

A rabbit who is in a basket and totally enjoying a carrot. *Mary Lou Holt collection.*

Gund rabbit, 1950s-1960s. *Joyce McClelland.*

Two circus rabbits who are dressed for the occasion. *Private collection.*

A candy container with two rabbits on top and a child in a rabbit suit carrying a basket. *Debrah Holt.*

An old rabbit sitting down for a rest after a long walk. *Mimi's Memories.*

A skier rabbit who still has to rent skis. *Mimi's Memories.*

Two Chenille rabbits, 1930s-1940s. *Curtis Smith.*

One air-activated hopping rabbit, and one made out of hide. *Mary Lou Holt collection.*

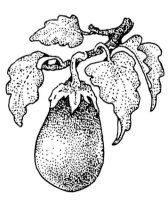

Wooden Rabbits

French carousel rabbit from the late 1800s or early 1900s who has just seen that his picture is going to be included in a book. *Schiffer Publishing collection*.

A box of blocks that tells about a rabbit. *Private collection.*

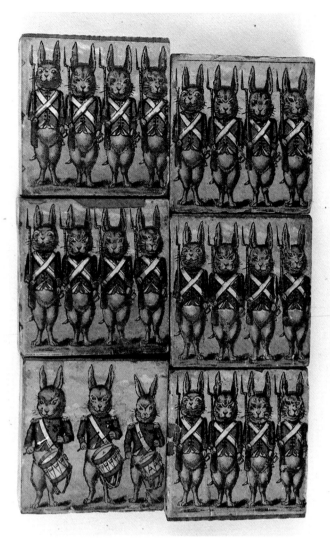

Wood blocks that are made to be used as toys. *Private collection.*

Two rabbit pull-toys that are to hold candy. *Private collection.*

Three wood cut-outs of field worker bunnies. *Private collection.*

Shoenhutt rebuilt, painted toy with jointed legs made of wood and his elegant trainer. *Margaret Schiffer collection.*

Four more wood cut-outs of rabbit field workers. *Private collection.*

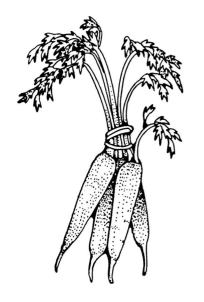

One paper and one tin container, a wood cut-out, and a plastic toy. *Mary Lou Holt collection.*

A wood basket made with cut-out rabbits on both ends. *Lare.*

Two candy container rabbits that are attached to carts. *Mary Lou Holt collection.*

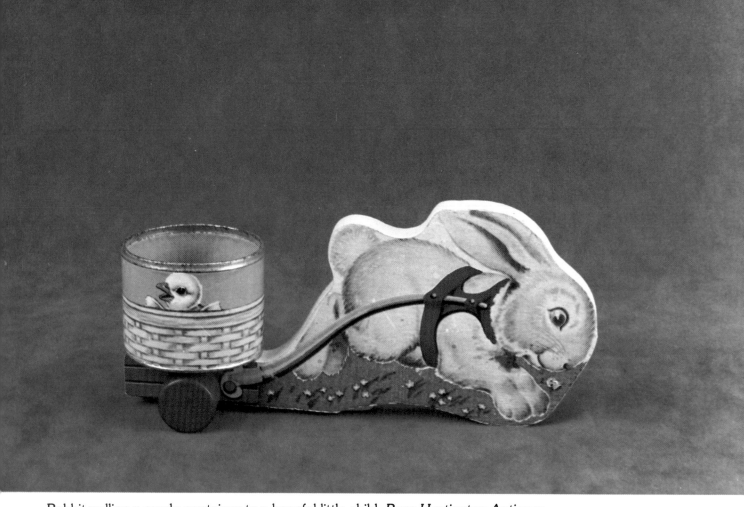

Rabbit pulling a candy container to a hopeful little child. *Russ Hartington Antiques, Toys.*

A little rabbit pounding on his drum to signal the start of Easter dinner. *Russ Hartington Antiques, Toys.*

Two bunnies bringing eggs form an Easter mobile.

Three rabbits carved by Tom Wolfe out of wood. *Tom Wolfe.*

Two young, inquisitive bunnies carved by Rosalyn Leach Daisey out of wood. *Rosalyn Leach Daisey.*

Paper game where you throw a ring around the rabbit. *Debrah Holt.*

German papier-maché candy box. *Margaret Schiffer collection.*

Uncle Wiggily Game. *Mary Lou Holt collection.*

Paper Rabbits

Paper advertisement for a type of bacon. *Mary Lou Holt collection.*

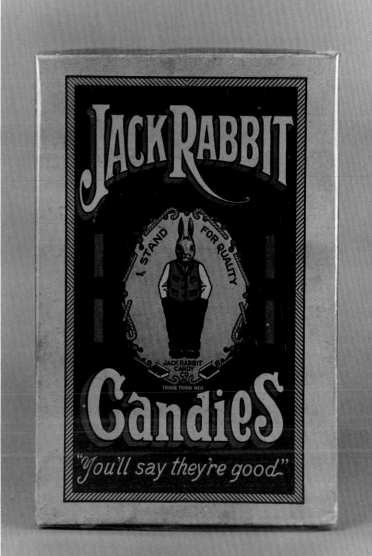

Jack Rabbit candy box. *Mary Lou Holt collection.*

Two paper cut-out rabbits. *Boyd Hitchner.*

An advertisement for a type of ham. *Mary Lou Holt collection.*

A paper cut-out advertisement for ham and bacon. *Mary Lou Holt collection.*

A card you put in front of a light and presto, a rabbit shadow. *Private collection.*

An old picture involving a rabbit **skin**. *Private collection.*

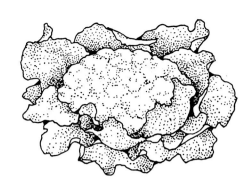

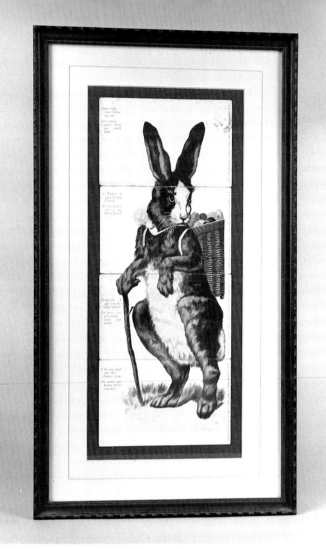

A four-part Easter bunny picture. *Mary Lou Holt collection.*

A paper advertisement for men's clothes. *Mary Lou Holt collection.*

Late nineteenth-century Christmas scene. *Margaret Schiffer collection.*

Two figures of rabbits in baskets. *Mary Lou Holt collection.*

Paper figure of a rabbit. The yellow paper folds down and forms a screen of paper. *Private collection.*

Similar, but the screen is down. *Private collection.*

Easter egg to be hung on a tree. *Private collection.*

Three greeting cards. *Private collection.*

A little scene with rabbits and chicks. *Private collection.*

Two greeting cards that are meant for Easter. *Private collection.*

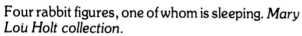

Six rabbit heads used as greeting cards. *Private collection.*

Four rabbit figures, one of whom is sleeping. *Mary Lou Holt collection.*

Paper Dresden rabbits. *Margaret Schiffer collection.*

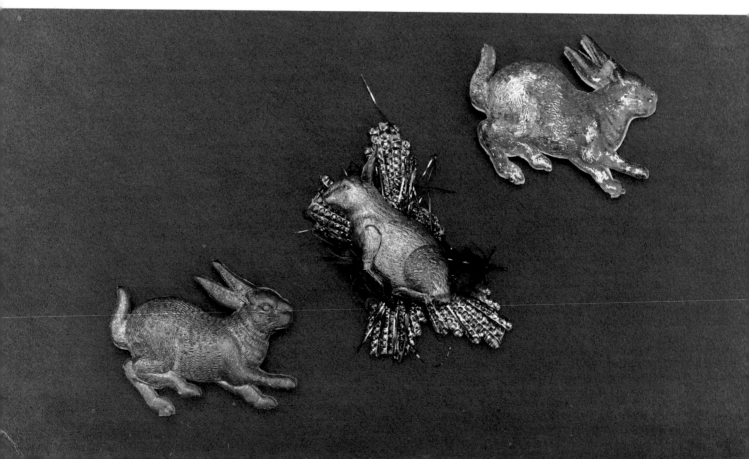

Papier-Maché Rabbits

A green Easter egg with animals on it. *Fran and Jim Pohrer.*

Red papier-maché Easter eggs. *Margaret Schiffer collection.*

A boy on a rabbit coming out of an egg. *Fran and Jim Pohrer.*

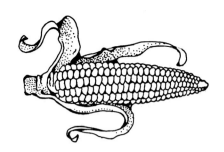

A rabbit in a green outfit with a red tricycle. *Private collection.*

A rabbit pulling a cart with an egg inside. *Mary Lou Holt collection.*

Three rabbits, one with no wagon and two with them. *Mary Lou Holt collection.*

One papier-maché and one cast rabbit. *Fran and Jim Pohrer.*

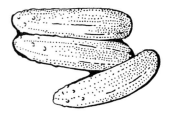

Three papier-maché rabbit gentlemen. *Margaret Schiffer collection.*

Two German squeak toys and one pull toy. *Margaret Schiffer collection.*

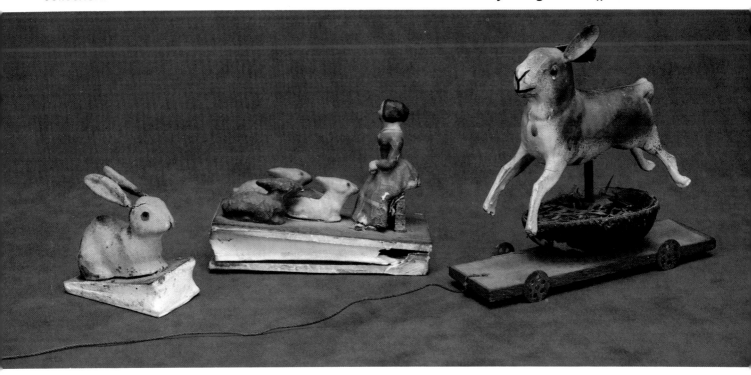

Three rabbits, the one to the left has a spring neck. *Fran and Jim Pohrer*.

Opposite:
A sitting rabbit. *Mary Lou Holt collection*.

Two rabbits, one is walking a great distance and the other is used as a horse. *Bierdman collection*.

A family of rabbits. *Private collection*.

A bunny that is in the tree to get a better view. *Private collection.*

Candy container rabbit with his lunch on his back. *Mary Lou Holt collection.*

A German golf papier-maché candy container. *Curtis Smith.*

Three papier-maché rabbits. *Margaret Schiffer collection.*

Three rabbits, and the left one is still in his shell. *Fran and Jim Pohrer.*

A family of rabbits all posing for the picture. *Fran and Jim Pohrer.*

Three dressed papier-maché rabbit figures coming in from the field. *Margaret Schiffer collection.*

Papier-maché advertising rabbit. *Bunny Walker*.

School boy candy container. *Scott Tagliapietra*.

The rabbit scientist has finally found a new kind of egg. *Mary Lou Holt collection*.

Papier-maché candy container. *Mary Lou Holt collection.*

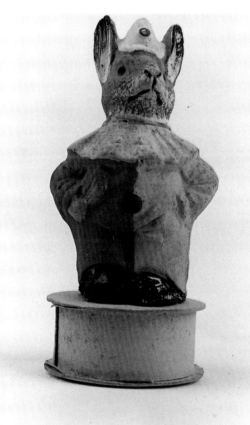

Another clown. *Private collection.*

Clown rabbit candy container. *Mary Lou Holt collection.*

Three little school children. *Mary Lou Holt collection.*

A rabbit peasant laborer. *Private collection.*

Three rabbits all
eating and talking
happily. *Private
collection.*

A worker and his employers. *Fran and Jim Pohrer*.

Three papier-maché candy containers. *Private collection*.

A rabbit candy container. *Mary Lou Holt collection*.

Rabbit returning from the chicken coop with eggs and yelling to his mother because they are already colored. *Hillman-Gemini Antiques*.

A small rabbit who is going somewhere formal. *Fran and Jim Pohrer.*

A rabbit that plays the drum for a band. *Bierdman collection.*

A white papier-maché rabbit with a big pink bow. *Bierdman collection.*

A family from the upper class. *Fran and Jim Pohrer.*

A rabbit about to show off to his friends. *Mary Lou Holt collection.*

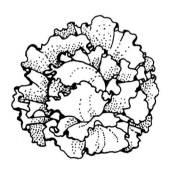

Two of three rabbits are in shells and the free one is being observant. *Bierdman collection.*

A goofy teacher is telling one of his pupils that he has to shape up. *Country Classiques*.

Large mother rabbit scolding her teenage son for being out too late. *Private collection*.

Three siblings wondering where their brother found his carrot. *Fran and Jim Pohrer*.

A rabbit trying to stand on the ball. *Private collection.*

A young rabbit maiden alighting from an egg shell. *Fran and Jim Pohrer.*

Two rabbit trainers are sad because they got stuck in shells. *Betty and R.C. Hursman.*

A brown papier-maché rabbit.

Papier-maché rabbit figures. *Margaret Schiffer collection.*

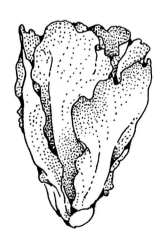

A group of rabbit field workers.

The two most prominent figures of their community. *Fran and Jim Pohrer.*

Two papier-maché rabbit figures hoarding Easter eggs. *Mary Lou Holt collection.*

Three Easter rabbits made out of papier-maché. *Private collection.*

An Easter rabbit all ready to be given to some deserving little child. *Mary Lou Holt collection.*

Six books about rabbits (note that some are cloth.) *Mary Lou Holt collection.*

Books for Rabbits

This book is made out of cloth and it is still in good condition. *Private collection.*

These two books are about nice rabbits. *Mary Lou Holt collection.*

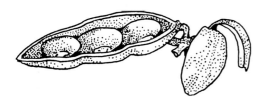

This book is about a bunny family. *Mary Lou Holt collection.*

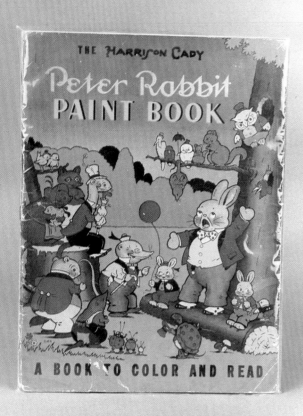

This is a book that you are supposed to paint. *Mary Lou Holt collection.*

Another cloth book, but look at Peter—he has a basket. *Private collection.*